PRIMARY SOURCES OF
FAMOUS PEOPLE IN AMERICAN HISTORY™

BETSY ROSS

CREATOR OF THE AMERICAN FLAG
CREADORA DE LA BANDERA ESTADOUNIDENSE

JENNIFER SILATE

TRADUCCIÓN AL ESPAÑOL:
EIDA DE LA VEGA

rosen central
Primary Source™
Editorial Buenas Letras™

The Rosen Publishing Group, Inc., New York

Published in 2004 by The Rosen Publishing Group, Inc.
29 East 21st Street, New York, NY 10010

First Bilingual Edition 2004
First English Edition 2004

Cataloging Data

Silate, Jennifer.
[Betsy Ross. Bilingual]
Betsy Ross / by Jennifer Silate. —1st ed.
    p. cm. — (Grandes personajes en la historia de los Estados Unidos)
Summary: Introduces the life of Betsy Ross, an American patriot during the Revolutionary War who enjoyed telling her family about how she sewed the first American flag.
Includes bibliographical references (p.) and index.
ISBN 0-8239-4152-3(lib. bdg.)
1. Ross, Betsy, 1752-1836—Juvenile literature. 2. Revolutionaries—United States—Biography—Juvenile literature. 3. United States—History—Revolution, 1775-1783—Flags—Juvenile literature. 4. Flags—United States—History—18th century—Juvenile literature. [1. Ross, Betsy, 1752-1836. 2. Revolutionaries. 3. United States—History—Revolution, 1775-1783. 4. Flags—United States. 5. Women—Biography. 6. Spanish language materials bilingual.]
I. Title. II. Series. Primary sources of famous people in American history. Bilingual
E302.6.R77S57 2003
973.3'092—dc21
[B]

Manufactured in the United States of America

Photo credits: Cover © Bettmann/Corbis; p. 5 Courtesy of Charles H. Weisgerber II; p.7© North Wind Picture Archives; p. 9 Maura B. McConnell, courtesy Betsy Ross House; p. 11 © Lee Snider/Corbis; p. 13 Library of Congress Rare Books and Special Collections Division ; p.15 Print Collection, Miriam and Ira D. Wallach Division of Art, Prints and Photographs, The New York Public Library, Astor, Lennox and Tilden Foundations; pp. 17 (top), 23, 27 © Corbis; p. 17 (bottom) The Rosen Publishing Group; p. 19 © SuperStock, Inc.; p. 21 © The Granger Collection, New York ; p. 25 Courtesy of the American Philosophical Society, Records of the Society of Free Quakers; p. 29 The Harper's New Monthly Magazine

Designer: Thomas Forget; Editor: Jill Jarnow; Photo Researcher: Rebecca Anguin-Cohen

CONTENTS

CONTENIDO

1 YOUNG BETSY ROSS

Many people believe that Betsy Ross made the first American flag. But no one knows for sure. Whether or not she did, Betsy Ross was an unusual woman of her time.

She was born Elizabeth Griscom on January 1, 1752. Her nickname was Betsy. She lived with her family in West Jersey, Pennsylvania. Later, she became known as Betsy Ross.

---

1 LA JOVEN BETSY ROSS

Mucha gente cree que Betsy Ross hizo la primera bandera de Estados Unidos. Pero nadie lo sabe con certeza. Tanto si es verdad como si no, Betsy Ross fue una mujer excepcional. Se llamaba Elizabeth Griscom y nació el 1 de enero de 1752. Le decían Betsy. Vivía con su familia en West Jersey, Pensilvania. Más tarde fue conocida como Betsy Ross.

Here is how an artist imagined Betsy Ross looked with the first American flag she sewed.

Así imaginó un artista a Betsy Ross mientras cosía la bandera de Estados Unidos.

The Griscoms were Quaker. Quakers believed in simple living. They did not believe in fighting or in war.

Quaker children did not play cards, listen to music, or dance. They played hide-and-seek and jumped rope.

Most girls in colonial times could not go to school. But Quaker girls did. At Quaker school Betsy learned to read, write, and sew.

Los Griscom eran cuáqueros. Los cuáqueros creían en la vida sencilla. No creían en peleas ni en guerras.

Los niños cuáqueros no jugaban a las cartas, no escuchaban música ni bailaban. Jugaban al escondite y a saltar a la cuerda.

La mayoría de las niñas en tiempos de los colonos no podían ir a la escuela, pero las niñas cuáqueras, sí. En la escuela cuáquera, Betsy aprendió a leer, a escribir y a coser.

This hand-colored engraving shows people at a Philadelphia Quaker meeting for worship.

Este grabado coloreado a mano muestra una reunión cuáquera en Filadelfia.

Betsy finished school when she was 12. She became an apprentice in an upholstery shop. Betsy lived and worked there.

John Ross was an apprentice in the same shop. Betsy and John fell in love. John and Betsy married on November 4, 1773. They opened their own upholstery shop.

Betsy terminó la escuela a los 12 años. Entró de aprendiza en un taller de tapicería. Betsy vivía y trabajaba allí.

John Ross era aprendiz en el mismo taller. Betsy y Ross se enamoraron y se casaron el 4 de noviembre de 1773. Juntos abrieron su propio taller de tapicería.

These old upholstery tools are on display in the Betsy Ross House in Philadelphia.

Estas antiguas herramientas de tapicería se exhiben en la Casa Betsy Ross en Filadelfia.

Quakers did not allow their members to marry people from other religions. John Ross was not a Quaker. Betsy's family was very angry when she married John. Quaker law said Betsy could no longer pray in the Quaker meetinghouse. So John and Betsy Ross attended Christ Church.

Los cuáqueros no permitían que los miembros de su familia se casaran con gente de otras religiones. John Ross no era cuáquero y la familia de Betsy se enojó cuando se casaron. La ley cuáquera no permitía que Betsy fuera a orar al templo cuáquero. De modo que John y Betsy Ross iban a la Iglesia de Cristo.

Betsy and John Ross attended Christ Church in Philadelphia. This church was built between 1722 and 1747.

Betsy y John asistían a la Iglesia de Cristo en Filadelfia. La iglesia fue construida entre 1722 y 1747.

Soon after John and Betsy were married, Paul Revere came to Philadelphia. He told everyone about the Boston Tea Party. The colonists did not want to pay Britain high taxes for tea. They protested by throwing tea into Boston Harbor. Some of the colonists were dressed like Mohawk Indians.

---

2 LA GUERRA DE INDEPENDENCIA

Poco después de casados, Paul Revere vino a Filadelfia, con la noticia de la Fiesta del Té de Boston. Los colonos no querían pagar los altos impuestos que los ingleses exigían por el té. Entonces protestaron lanzando un cargamento de té a la bahía de Boston. Algunos colonos estaban vestidos de indios Mohawk.

Americans throwing the Cargoes of the Tea Ships into the River, at Boston

Colonists throwing tea into Boston Harbor in 1773

Colonos lanzando té a la bahía de Boston en 1773

The colonists and the British began to fight the Revolutionary War. The first battles were near Boston in 1775. Betsy and John sided with the colonists. John joined the Pennsylvania militia. He guarded gunpowder. When it exploded, he was hurt badly. He died on January 21, 1776. Betsy decided to run the shop alone.

———◆———

Los colonos y los ingleses comenzaron la Guerra de Independencia. Las primeras batallas fueron cerca de Boston, en 1775. Betsy y John se unieron al bando de los colonos. John se unió a la milicia de Pensilvania. Estaba encargado de custodiar el polvorín. Cuando éste explotó, John quedó gravemente herido. Murió el 21 de enero de 1776. Betsy decidió administrar sola la tapicería.

Amos Doolittle engraved many pictures of the Battle of Lexington and Concord.

Amos Doolittle hizo grabados de imágenes de la batalla de Lexington y Concord.

3 THE FIRST AMERICAN FLAG

George Washington was the leader of the colonial army. He used a red-and-white striped flag. A small British flag was in the corner. When the British saw the flag, they thought he wanted to surrender. Washington decided the colonies needed a new flag.

---

3 LA PRIMERA BANDERA DE ESTADOS UNIDOS

George Washington era el líder del ejército revolucionario. Al principio de la guerra usó una bandera de franjas rojas y blancas con una pequeña bandera inglesa en una esquina. Cuando los ingleses vieron la bandera, pensaron que Washington quería rendirse, así que éste decidió que las colonias necesitaban una nueva bandera.

George Washington and a copy of the flag he first used to call his troops together

George Washington y una copia de la primera bandera bajo la que reunió a sus tropas

George Washington, George Ross, and Robert Morris were on the flag committee. They went to Betsy's shop with an idea for the first American flag. It had thirteen stars, one for each colony. The stars had six points. Betsy suggested using stars with five points. They agreed.

They asked her to make the flag. Betsy was very proud.

George Washington, George Ross y Robert Morris pertenecían al comité que creó la bandera. Fueron al taller de Betsy con una idea para el diseño de la primera bandera de Estados Unidos. Tenía trece estrellas, una por cada colonia. Las estrellas tenían seis puntas. Betsy les sugirió utilizar estrellas de cinco puntas. Todos estuvieron de acuerdo.

Le pidieron a Betsy que hiciera la bandera. Betsy se sintió muy orgullosa.

This is what it might have been like when Betsy Ross presented her American flag to the flag committee.

Esta pintura muestra a Betsy Ross presentando la bandera de Estados Unidos al comité.

4 SOLDIERS IN PHILADELPHIA

In 1777, Betsy married Joseph Ashburn, a sailor. He was often at sea. Betsy ran the shop.

Battles were getting close to Philadelphia. In September 1777, the British entered Philadelphia.

British soldiers took whatever they wanted from the colonists. Soldiers even moved into Betsy's house.

---

4 SOLDADOS EN FILADELFIA

En 1777, Betsy se casó con Joseph Ashburn, un marinero que casi siempre estaba en el mar. Betsy administraba el taller cuando la guerra se acercaba a Filadelfia. En septiembre de 1777, los ingleses entraron a la ciudad.

Los soldados ingleses tomaron todo lo que se les antojó de los colonos. Algunos soldados incluso se instalaron en la casa de Betsy.

During the 1777 Battle of Germantown, colonists tried to force the British out. There was a bloody fight. The colonists lost.

Durante la batalla de Germantown en 1777, los colonos trataron de expulsar a los ingleses. Hubo una sangrienta lucha. Los colonos perdieron.

In 1778, the French entered the American war against the British. The British were afraid the French might attack New York City. They left Philadelphia to guard it.

In 1779, Betsy and Joseph's first daughter was born. Her name was Zillah. The next year, Joseph left to get war supplies. Soon after, Betsy had another daughter named Eliza.

En 1778, los franceses se unieron a la lucha contra los ingleses. Los ingleses temían que los franceses atacaran la ciudad de Nueva York. Abandonaron Filadelfia para proteger Nueva York.

En 1779, nació la primera hija de Betsy y Joseph. Le pusieron Zillah. Al año siguiente, Joseph se marchó para obtener suministros para la guerra. Muy poco después, nació Eliza, su segunda hija.

The Declaration of Independence was signed in 1776. This map is called *The Seat of War in the Northern Colonies.*

La Declaración de Independencia se firmó en 1776, en Filadelfia. Este mapa se llama *Enclave de la guerra en las colonias del norte.*

5 AFTER THE WAR

The war ended in 1781. John Claypoole returned from England. He had been a war prisoner with Joseph, Betsy's husband. He told Betsy that Joseph had died.

John Claypoole and Betsy became good friends. They were married in 1783. John helped Betsy run the upholstery shop. Together they had five daughters.

---

5 DESPUÉS DE LA GUERRA

La guerra terminó en 1781. John Claypoole regresó de Inglaterra. Había sido prisionero de guerra junto con Joseph, el esposo de Betsy. Le contó a Betsy que Joseph había muerto. John Claypoole y Betsy se hicieron buenos amigos. Se casaron en 1783. John ayudó a Betsy a administrar el taller de tapicería. Tuvieron cinco hijas.

Joseph Warner — Charity Warner
William Darragh — Mary Lawn
Rowld Parry — Elizabeth Thomson
Samuel Eldredge — Lidia Crispin
T. Matlack — Elizabeth Neave
Jonathan Scholfield — Elizabeth Neave Junr
Rebecah Scholfield — Hannah Carmalt
Jacob Lahn — Elizabeth Claypoole
William Thomson — Margorita Räefrewin
Samuel Crispin Senior — Sarah Wetherill Daughter of
William Milnor — Samuel Wetherill & Sarah his Wife
Eli Lewis — Mary Crispin for order
Wm. Matlack — Martha Wetherby Jr order
Samuel Wetherill Minr — Thomas Lang — Margaret
Alord Wetherill — Wife of Thomas Lang and
John Wetherill — Margaret Lang his
Rachl Somers — daughter
William Smallwood — James Lang
John Claypoole — Mary Elton
Jacob Räefer — Susannah Elton
George Kemble — John Elton
Thomas Elton — Thomas Elton
 — Elizabeth Elton
 — Anthony Elton

Children of Thomas Elton

Betsy and John Claypoole joined the Society of Free Quakers. Betsy signed the membership book in 1785.

Betsy y John Claypoole entraron en la Sociedad de Cuáqueros Libres. Betsy firmó el libro de miembros en 1785.

John and Betsy were married for a long time. They were always very busy.

John Claypoole died in 1817.

Betsy retired in 1827. Her daughter and a niece ran the shop. Betsy lived with another daughter.

Betsy Ross died on January 30, 1836. She was 84 years old.

John y Betsy estuvieron casados mucho tiempo. Siempre estaban muy ocupados. John Claypoole murió en 1817.

Betsy se retiró en 1827. Su hija y una sobrina admistraban el taller. Betsy vivía con otra hija.

Betsy Ross murió el 30 de enero de 1836. Tenía 84 años.

Betsy Ross rented this house from 1773 to 1786 for her upholstery shop.

Betsy Ross alquiló esta casa desde 1773 hasta 1786 para usarla como taller de tapicería.

6   BETSY'S LEGACY

Betsy Ross had often told her family how she made the first American flag. In 1870, her grandson and other relatives told Betsy's story to the Historical Society of Pennsylvania. There is no other proof.

   We don't know if Betsy sewed the first American flag. One thing is certain. Betsy Ross is a true American hero.

---

6   EL LEGADO DE BETSY

Con frecuencia, Betsy Ross le contaba a su familia cómo hizo la primera bandera de Estados Unidos. En 1870, su nieto y otros parientes le relataron la historia a la Sociedad Histórica de Pensilvania. Ésta es la única prueba que existe.

   No sabemos si Betsy cosió la primera bandera de Estados Unidos. Pero una cosa es cierta. Betsy Ross es una verdadera heroína norteamericana.

MRS. ROSS AND THE FLAG COMMITTEE.

sary for the purpose of signals, Colonel Moultrie, who was requested by the Council of Safety to procure one, had a large blue flag made, with a crescent in one corner, to be uniform with the troops.

October 20, 1775, Colonel Reed, with the co-operation of Colonels Glover and Moylan, designed a flag or signal to be used by the American cruisers, which was adopted. It is described as a white flag with a pine-tree in the centre, and bearing the motto, "Appeal to Heaven." The London *Chronicle*, an anti-ministerial paper, contains a paragraph, January, 1776, describing a flag of this description captured with a provincial privateer at that time.

"February 9, 1776, Colonel Gadsden presented to Congress an elegant standard, such as is to be used by the commander-in-chief of the American navy, being a yellow field, with a lively representation of a rattlesnake in the middle in the attitude of going to strike, and the words underneath, 'Don't tread on me.'

"*Ordered*, That the said standard be carefully preserved and suspended in the Congress-room."

Several accounts lead to the belief that at the battle of Bunker Hill standards of various devices were used by the patriot army. From one statement we learn that "the Americans displayed a flag with the cross of St. George, the ground being blue, and in the upper corner nearest the staff a pine-tree." Another writer says that Bunker Hill was fought under a red flag, bearing the motto, "Come, if you dare."

On the 14th of June, 1777, Congress took action, viz.: "*Resolved*, That the flag of the United States be thirteen stripes alternately red and white; that the *union be thirteen stars, white in a blue field, representing a new constellation.*" It was also proposed to insert a lyre, about which the thirteen stars were to be grouped, as embodying the "constellation Lyra," signifying harmony. But this suggestion was not carried out.

The blue field was taken from the Covenanters' banner in Scotland, likewise significant of the league and covenant of the United Colonies against oppression, and incidentally involving vigilance, perseverance, and justice. The stars were then disposed in a circle, symbolizing the perpetuity of the Union, the circle being the sign of eternity. The thirteen stripes showed with the stars the number of the United Colonies, and denoted the subordination of the States to and their dependence upon the Union, as well as equality with themselves. The whole was a blending of the various flags used previous to the war, viz., the red flags of the army and white colors of the floating batteries—the germ of our navy. The red color also, which, with the Romans, was the emblem of defiance, denoted daring, and the white purity.

The five-pointed star, from the heraldry

An article in *Harper's New Monthly Magazine* says Betsy showed Washington how to make a five-pointed star.

Un artículo de Harper's Monthly dice que Betsy le enseñó a Washington a hacer una estrella de cinco puntas.

TIMELINE

January 1, 1752—Elizabeth (Betsy) Griscom is born.

1775—Revolutionary War begins.

1827—Betsy stops working at her upholstery shop.

1870—William Canby, a grandson, makes Betsy's story known.

1764—Betsy becomes an apprentice in an upholstery shop.

1776—Betsy makes the first American flag.

1836—Betsy Ross dies.

CRONOLOGÍA

1 de enero de 1752—Nace Elizabeth (Betsy) Griscom.

1775—Comienza la Guerra de Independencia.

1827—Betsy se retira de su taller de tapicería.

1870—William Canby, un nieto de Betsy, cuenta la historia de la primera bandera.

1764—Betsy entra de aprendiza en un taller de tapicería.

1776—Betsy hace la primera bandera de Estados Unidos.

1836—Betsy Ross muere.

30

GLOSSARY

apprentice (uh-PREN-tis) A person who learns a trade by working for an experienced person.

Historical Society of Pennsylvania (hih-STOR-ih-kul suh-SYE-ih-tee UV pen-sul-VAYN-yuh) A group that gathers information about the history of Pennsylvania.

militia (muh-LISH-uh) A group of citizens who are trained to fight but who only serve in times of emergency.

Revolutionary War (re-vuh-LOO-shuh-ner-ee WOR) The war (1775–1781) in which the first thirteen American colonies won their independence from Great Britain.

upholstery shop (uhp-HOHL-stur-ee SHOP) A store where clothes, curtains, chairs, and other things were sewn.

WEB SITES

Due to the changing nature of Internet links, the Rosen Publishing Group, Inc., has developed an online list of Web sites related to the subject of this book. This site is updated regularly. Please use this link to access the list:

http://www.rosenlinks.com/fpah/bros

GLOSARIO

aprendiz (a) Una persona que aprende un oficio trabajando con una persona experimentada.

Guerra de Independencia (la) Guerra (1775–1781) en la que las primeras trece colonias de Norteámerica se independizaron de Inglaterra.

milicia (la) Un grupo de ciudadanos entrenados para luchar, pero que sólo son usados en emergencias.

Sociedad Histórica de Pensilvania (la) Un grupo que colecciona información acerca de la historia de Pensilvania.

taller de tapicería (el) Una tienda donde se cosen sillas, cortinas, ropas y otras cosas.

SITIOS WEB

Debido a las constantes modificaciones en los sitios de Internet, Rosen Publishing Group, Inc. ha desarrollado un listado de sitios Web relacionados con el tema de este libro. Este sitio se actualiza con regularidad. Por favor, usa este enlace para acceder a la lista:

http://www.rosenlinks.com/fpah/bros

INDEX

ABOUT THE AUTHOR

Jennifer Silate lives and writes on her boat in Maryland.

ÍNDICE

ACERCA DEL AUTOR

Jennifer Silate vive y escribe en su barco en Maryland.